The Science of Living Things

What is a Fish?

Bobbie Kalman & Allison Larin

Crabtree Publishing Company
www.crabtreebooks.com

The Science of Living Things Series
A Bobbie Kalman Book

**To Stephanie Crooke,
for having such a great sense of humor.**

Editor-in-Chief
Bobbie Kalman

Writing team
Bobbie Kalman
Allison Larin

Managing editor
Lynda Hale

Project editor
Heather Levigne

Research and editing team
April Fast
Kate Calder
Jane Lewis
John Crossingham
Hannelore Sotzek

Computer design
Lynda Hale

**Production coordinator
and photo researcher**
Hannelore Sotzek

Special thanks to
Rodger Moody and Ryan Carter

Photographs
EarthWater: Craig Cook: page 9 (top); Chris Crumley: page 13
Tom Stack & Associates: Dave Fleetham: pages 10, 19 (top), 25 (middle),
    30 (bottom); Jeff Foott: page 23 (all); Brian Parker: page 17 (top);
    Denise Tackett: page 21 (inset); Larry Tackett: pages 4-5, 9 (bottom);
    Denise & Larry Tackett: page 9 (middle); Tom Stack: page 19 (bottom)
Valan Photos: Jean Bruneau: page 30 (top); Paul L. Janosi: page 28
    (bottom left)
Norbert Wu: pages 12, 15 (bottom), 17 (bottom), 20-21, 22, 25 (top),
    26 (both), 27 (both), 29 (bottom)
Other photographs by Digital Stock and Digital Vision

Illustrations
Barbara Bedell: page 18
Cori Marvin: pages 6-7, 10, 11, 13
Bonna Rouse: page 8

Crabtree Publishing Company

www.crabtreebooks.com   1-800-387-7650

Cataloging in Publication Data
Kalman, Bobbie
    What is a fish?
(The science of living things)
Includes index.
ISBN 0-86505-882-2 (library bound) ISBN 0-86505-894-6 (pbk.)
This book introduces fishes, showing and describing different types, including
freshwater and saltwater, and discussing their anatomy, habitats,
reproduction, and diet.
1. Fishes—Juvenile literature. [1. Fishes.] I. Larin, Allison. II. Title.
III. Series: Kalman, Bobbie. Science of living things
QL617.2.K35 1999   j597   LC 98-41881
                                                                        CIP

**Published in
the United States**
PMB16A
350 Fifth Ave.
Suite 3308
New York, NY
10118

**Published
in Canada**
616 Welland Ave.,
St. Catharines, Ontario
Canada
L2M 5V6

**Published in the
United Kingdom**
73 Lime Walk
Headington
Oxford
OX3 7AD
United Kingdom

**Published
in Australia**
386 Mt. Alexander Rd.,
Ascot Vale (Melbourne)
VIC 3032

Contents

What is a fish?

Fish are animals that live their entire lives under water. They are **vertebrate** animals, which means they have a backbone. Birds, reptiles, and humans are all vertebrates. Fish do not have legs for moving around. They use their **fins** to swim through water. Fish breathe under water through **gills** instead of lungs.

Cold-blooded animals

Most fish are **cold-blooded**. Their body temperature changes with the temperature of the water in which they live. Birds and mammals are **warm-blooded**. Their body temperature stays the same no matter how warm or cold the environment is around them.

Salty or fresh

Most **species**, or types, of fish live in oceans. The water in oceans is **salt water**. The water in rivers and lakes is not salty. It is **fresh water**. Most fish that live in one type of water cannot live in the other type of water. Only a few species of fish can live in both.

*These red soldierfish swim together in a group for protection. A group of fish traveling together is called a **school**.*

Fish features:

- Fish live under water.
- All fish have a skeleton and spinal cord.
- Most fish are cold-blooded.
- Fish breathe under water using gills.
- They use fins to swim through water.

Kings of the sea

There are over 30 000 species of fish. There are more types of fish than all the other species of vertebrates put together. Fish have been on the earth longer than any other vertebrates—over 400 million years!

Fish groups

There are three major groups of fish—**bony fish, cartilaginous fish**, and **jawless fish**. Each group is different from the others in several ways.

Bony fish

Bony fish make up the largest group of fish. These fish have a skeleton made of bone. Their body is covered with smooth scales for protection. Bony fish have good eyesight, but their sense of smell is not as good as that of fish in the other groups. Salmon, angelfish, and tuna are all bony fish.

This lionfish is a bony fish. Its skeleton is made of hard bones like yours. There are more species of bony fish in the oceans than any other fish.

Cartilaginous fish

Cartilaginous fish have a skeleton made of a strong, flexible material called **cartilage**. Parts of your nose and ears are made of cartilage. Cartilaginous fish have skin that is covered with rough scales. They are fast swimmers. They do not have good eyesight, but they do have a good sense of smell. Sharks, rays, and skates are cartilaginous fish.

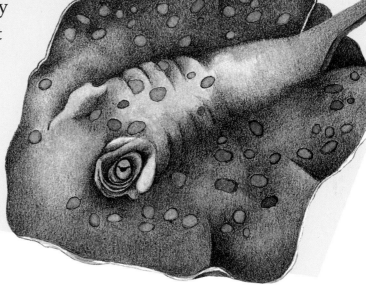

The stingray is a cartilaginous fish that protects itself with a sharp, poisonous spine on its tail.

Hagfish have slippery skin so they can crawl inside their prey in order to eat it.

Jawless fish

Jawless fish also have a skeleton made of cartilage, but their body is different from that of cartilaginous fish. Jawless fish have smooth, slimy skin with no scales. They do not have a jaw, so they cannot bite or chew. They just suck in their food! Jawless fish are not good swimmers. Lampreys and hagfish are examples of jawless fish.

Fish bodies

The body of a fish is suited to life under water. It is **fusiform**, or torpedo-shaped, to move quickly through the water. Fish have a brain, heart, backbone, liver, and many other body parts that you have as well. Like most living things, fish need food and a type of gas called **oxygen** to live. Fish use gills for breathing.

The **lateral line** runs along both sides of a fish. It allows the fish to sense differences in the water, such as current or pressure changes. The lateral line helps a fish stay oriented.

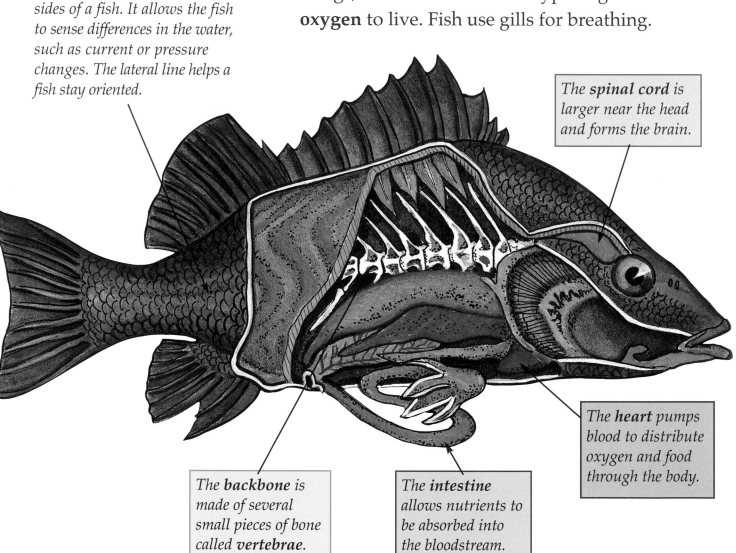

The **spinal cord** is larger near the head and forms the brain.

The **heart** pumps blood to distribute oxygen and food through the body.

The **backbone** is made of several small pieces of bone called **vertebrae**.

The **intestine** allows nutrients to be absorbed into the bloodstream.

Most fish have teeth. Their teeth are suited to the type of food they eat. Sharks eat other fish, so their teeth are large and sharp. The teeth of this parrotfish are made for breaking off, crushing, and eating pieces of coral.

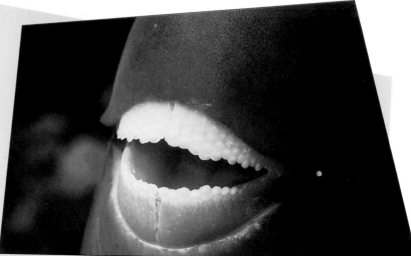

Fish never close their eyes because they do not have eyelids. Animals that live on land have eyelids to keep their eyeballs moist with liquid. Fish live in water, so they do not need eyelids to keep their eyeballs wet. These eyeballs belong to a peacock sole.

Scales

Most fish have scales that cover and protect their delicate skin. Fish scales can be different colors, shapes, and sizes. The scales covering the skin of a parrotfish change color as the fish becomes an adult.

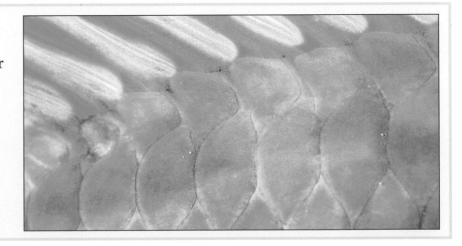

Water breathers

Animals need oxygen to stay alive. Humans and other land animals breathe air to get oxygen. Fish get oxygen from water. Instead of breathing through lungs, a fish uses gills to absorb oxygen. It also uses its gills to release carbon dioxide, which is another type of gas.

Fish such as this trumpet fish have nostrils, but they are used only for smelling and not for breathing.

Inhaling

A fish **inhales**, or breathes in, by sucking water into its mouth. Water runs down the throat and over the **gill filaments** in the gills. Gill filaments are covered with blood vessels that absorb oxygen from the water. Blood travels from these filaments and distributes oxygen throughout the body of the fish.

Exhaling

To **exhale**, or breathe out, a fish closes its mouth. Its throat becomes smaller, pushing the water out through its gills. The action of inhaling and exhaling moves water in through the mouth, down the throat, past the gills, and out of the body.

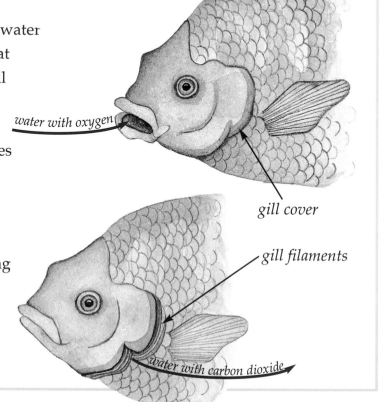

water with oxygen

gill cover

gill filaments

water with carbon dioxide

Guarding gills

Bony fish have flaps of skin over their gills called **opercula**, or gill covers. These covers protect the delicate gill filaments of a fish. Gill filaments can be torn or damaged by objects in the water such as sharp coral reefs or even other fish. Gill covers are also important for breathing. A fish tightly closes its gill covers when it inhales to keep the oxygen-rich water in its throat.

*Cartilaginous and jawless fish have openings called **gill slits**. As they swim, water flows through the gill slits and into the gills. If this shark stops swimming, it will not get enough oxygen to survive.*

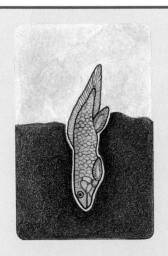 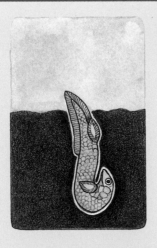 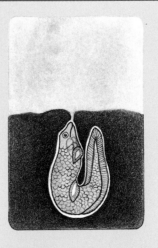 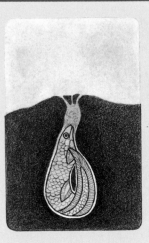

Fish with lungs

Some fish have both lungs and gills. These unique fish are called **lungfish**. Lungfish live in Africa, Australia, and South America, where hot weather sometimes causes rivers to dry up. Lungfish survive by burying themselves in the mud at the bottom of a river and breathing air with their lungs. They live in the mud until it rains and the river fills up again with water. Then they breathe under water with their gills.

How do fish swim?

Fish bodies are designed for swimming. Their **streamlined**, or sleek, body glides easily through water. Fish are covered with **mucus**. Mucus is a slimy substance that seeps out of their skin. It allows fish to swim smoothly through the water.

Fish use their fins for swimming. Fins can be different shapes and sizes. They are located at the top, sides, and tail of a fish. Each type of fin has a different purpose. Some fins help **camouflage** fish by blending in with the environment.

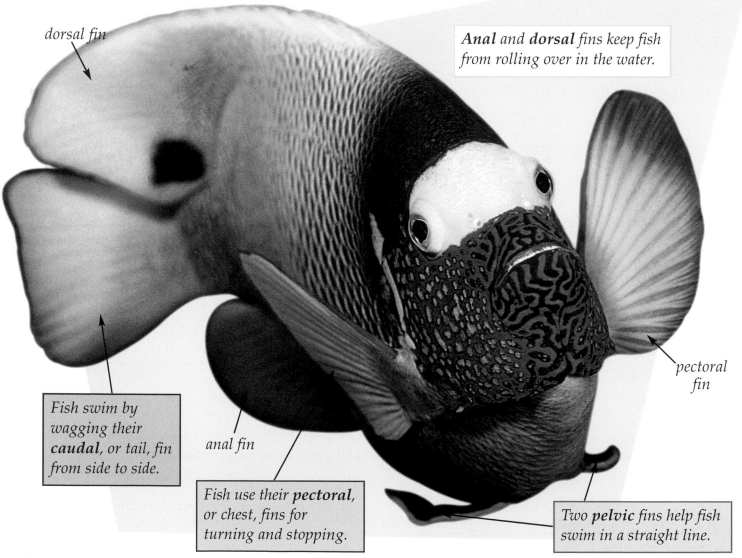

dorsal fin

Anal and dorsal fins keep fish from rolling over in the water.

*Fish swim by wagging their **caudal**, or tail, fin from side to side.*

anal fin

*Fish use their **pectoral**, or chest, fins for turning and stopping.*

pectoral fin

*Two **pelvic** fins help fish swim in a straight line.*

Swimming muscles

Fish have strong muscles along their sides to help them swim quickly. They wiggle their body in an S-pattern the way a snake does. Their tail presses against the water and pushes them forward. The faster they wiggle and wag, the faster they move through the water. Manta rays use muscle power to flap their large, winglike pectoral fins.

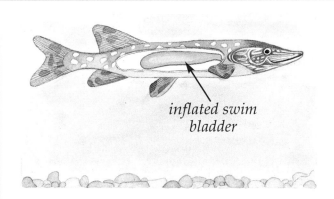

inflated swim bladder

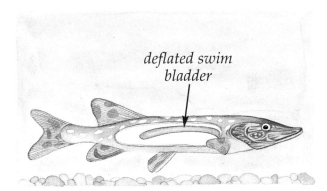

deflated swim bladder

Keeping afloat

Many fish have a **swim bladder**. A swim bladder is a sac inside the body of a fish that looks like a balloon. The air inside helps the fish stay afloat. When a fish **inflates** its swim bladder with air, the fish rises toward the surface of the water.

When the swim bladder is **deflated**, the fish sinks lower in the water. Fish that live in deep water or those that swim very fast do not have swim bladders. These fish have more fat on their body to keep them afloat. Fat floats because it is lighter than water.

Fish homes

Natural homes, such as rivers, are called **habitats**. Some fish live in freshwater habitats, and others live in saltwater homes. Some habitats are cold and dark, whereas others are warm and bright. Different types of fish need different water currents and temperatures. Fish also need different kinds and amounts of food to keep them alive.

Rivers and lakes

Freshwater fish live in rivers, lakes, ponds, and swamps. Most bodies of fresh water are shallower than salt water. Sunlight shines down onto the muddy bottom, helping plants grow. Plants are a rich source of food for many freshwater fish. Trout, perch, carp, and eels live in freshwater habitats.

Oceans

Oceans are made up of three parts—the **shallow sea**, **open sea**, and **deep sea**. Some fish live in the shallow sea year round. Others come only at certain times of the year to find food or have babies. Sea perch, plaice, skates, sunfish, and some sharks live in shallow seas.

The open sea is far from shore. Open-sea fish travel long distances to search for food, safety, and the right temperature and light. Sharks, rays, and many bony fish live in the open sea.

Some deep-sea fish have large eyes to help them see in the dark, but fish that live in the deepest part of the ocean have very small eyes or no eyes at all!

Deep sea

The deep sea is cold, dark, and quiet. Little sunlight reaches this ocean level so few plants and animals live there. Food can be difficult to find. Many deep-sea fish can eat prey larger than themselves. It may be a long time before a fish finds its next meal. Hatchetfish, viperfish, and gulper eels live in the deep sea.

The anglerfish has small eyes because its deep-ocean habitat has little light. It traps food with built-in "bait" that dangles over its mouth like bait on a fishing rod.

Life in a tropical reef

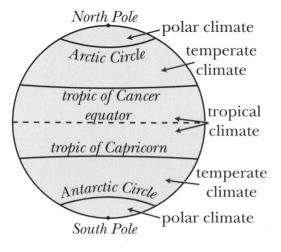

North Pole
polar climate
Arctic Circle
temperate climate
tropic of Cancer
equator
tropical climate
tropic of Capricorn
temperate climate
Antarctic Circle
polar climate
South Pole

Many types of colorful fish live in the warm waters around **tropical reefs**. Reefs are found in tropical areas of the world, where the climate is always warm. Tropical areas are close to the **equator**. The equator is an imaginary line that runs around the center of the earth. The equator and tropical areas receive more direct sunlight than other places on earth.

Coral homes

More types of sea creatures live in tropical reefs than in any other part of the ocean. A reef is a living thing too! It is made up of thousands of small, colorful sea creatures called **coral polyps**. Polyps grow on top of one another to form a coral reef. Fish and other sea animals find food and hide in the holes and crevices of a coral reef. Sea horses, angelfish, parrotfish, and clown fish live in tropical reefs.

*Many coral reef fish have stripes and spots to help camouflage them from **predators**. The patterns and colors of fish help them blend in with the brightly colored corals.*

Cleaning crew

A **goby** is a small tropical fish that feeds by cleaning larger fish that live in the coral reefs. The goby and other small cleaner fish eat **parasites** and dirt off the bodies of larger fish. They also clean out wounds. Some fish even let cleaners inside their mouth and gills!

Wrasses are also cleaners. This parrotfish is being cleaned by a wrasse. Clean skin helps the parrotfish stay healthy.

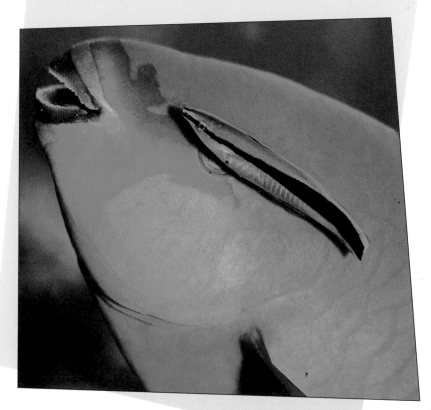

Fish food

Fish eat a variety of foods. Some fish are **herbivores** and eat only plants. Others eat animals. These fish are called **carnivores**. Many fish are **omnivores**. Omnivores eat both plants and animals.

Eat your vegetables!

Some fish eat **plankton**. Plankton are tiny plants and animals that float near the water's surface. Other fish eat **algae**, which are slimy living things that often grow on underwater rocks. Many large plants grow in fresh water, so most freshwater fish are herbivores or omnivores. Many freshwater fish also eat worms, freshwater shrimps, water fleas, and insects.

Meat eaters

Most ocean fish are carnivores. They eat fish or other ocean animals. Carnivorous fish such as sharks are skilled hunters that have sharp teeth and powerful jaws.

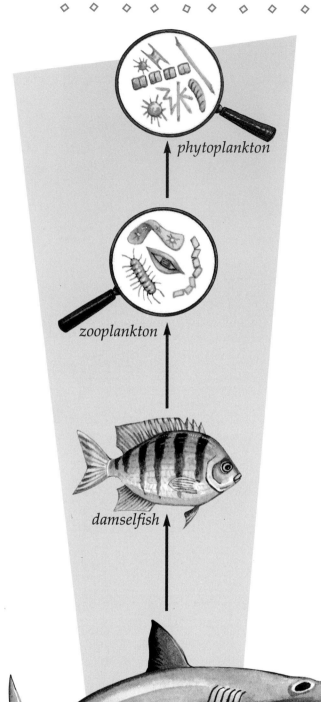

phytoplankton

zooplankton

damselfish

shark

The pattern of one living thing eating another is called a ***food chain***. *Every plant and animal belongs to at least one food chain. In this food chain, the shark eats the damselfish, which eats zooplankton, which feeds on phytoplankton.*

This devil scorpion fish is a carnivore. It is eating a butterfly fish. A butterfly fish is also a carnivore. It eats worms, sea slugs, and coral polyps.

Jawless fish food

Many jawless fish feed by attaching their mouth to the body of another fish. They suck nutrients from the other fish. Sometimes jawless fish can kill a fish by sucking too many nutrients from its body. These lampreys, shown left, have attached themselves to a carp.

Jawless fish have a mouth like a suction cup with many small teeth. The fish use it to latch onto other fish.

Mating and reproduction

Fish must **reproduce** so their species will survive. A male and female fish **mate** to produce more fish. Most species of fish lay eggs, but some fish keep the eggs inside their body until the babies are ready to be born.

Fertilization

Female fish produce many eggs. In order for those eggs to become fish, they must be **fertilized** by a male fish. Fertilization happens when the female's egg is joined with the male's **sperm**. Some female fish lay their eggs in the water to be fertilized. Other fish eggs are fertilized inside the body of the female.

Eggs

Many other fish and underwater animals eat fish eggs, so fish must lay many eggs at one time to make sure their species survives. Cod lay as many as seven million eggs! Freshwater fish, however, lay only a few hundred eggs at one time. Rivers and lakes do not contain as many fish and animals that eat fish eggs, so freshwater fish have a better chance of surviving.

In a tropical reef, these clown fish guard their eggs from predators.

Guarding eggs

Fish eggs are protected from predators in many different ways. Some male fish carry the fertilized eggs in a pouch on their stomach until they hatch. Other fish eggs float near the surface of the water where predators might not see them. Sometimes fish eggs grow in hard cases that float around on the waves.

Mouthbreeders carry their eggs around in their mouth until they hatch. This mouthbreeder is hiding in some coral. Look at all the eggs inside its mouth!

From egg to fish

Some eggs hatch in one or two days. Other eggs take up to five months to hatch. The larger the fish, the longer it takes for its eggs to hatch. Inside the egg is an **embryo**, or tiny baby, and a **yolk sac**. When a baby fish hatches, or breaks out of the egg, it is called a **larva**. At first it keeps the yolk sac on its belly and continues receiving nutrients from it. As the larva becomes larger, the yolk sac gets smaller. The larva soon begins to eat small plankton. It is now called a **fry**. Finally, the fry grows into an adult fish. It is ready to mate and lay eggs of its own.

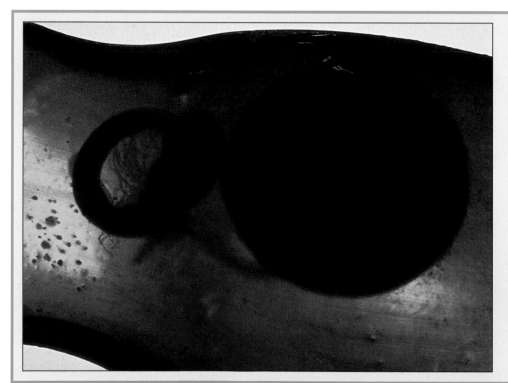

Egg cases

Most cartilaginous fish produce **live young**. A female fish carries eggs in her body, where they are fertilized by a male fish. Some fish release the eggs into the water in **egg cases**. The egg case protects the growing fish until it is ready to hatch. This shark egg case, shown left, holds an embryo.

1. A mature salmon mates with another adult salmon to reproduce. The female lays eggs, which are then fertilized by the male. 2. This salmon larva has just broken out of its egg. Not all the eggs hatch at once. Some of the nearby eggs have not yet hatched. 3. The yolk sac remains attached to the larva's belly to help it grow. 4. The larva grows larger and becomes a fry. The yolk sac has become smaller. A fry begins to search for its own food. The fry **matures**, or continues to grow, until it becomes an adult salmon.

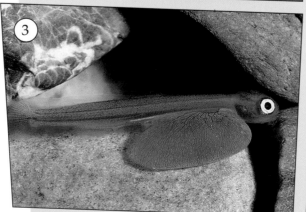

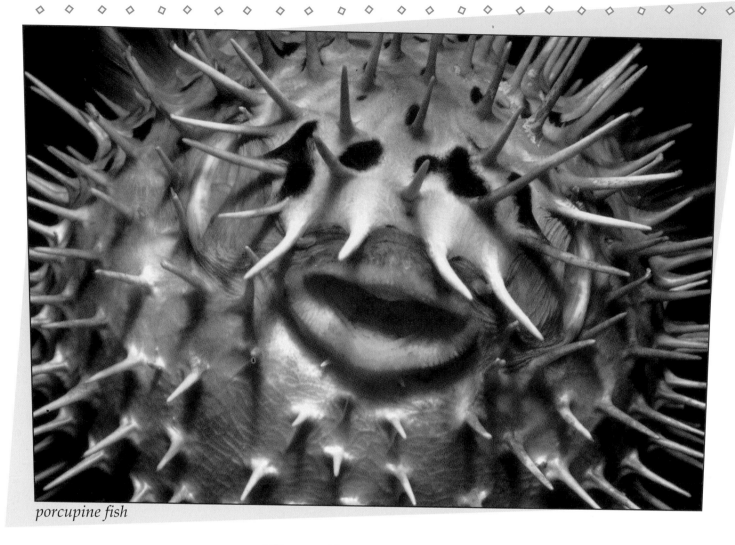
porcupine fish

Defenses

Fish have different ways of defending themselves against predators. Some fish use **warning coloration** to defend themselves. Their bright colors are a warning that these fish are dangerous to eat. Other fish can change colors to fool predators.

Puffer fish and porcupine fish protect themselves by making their body difficult to eat. When threatened, these fish quickly fill themselves with water. Their body puffs up, and their prickly spines stick straight out. Not many predators want a mouthful of spines!

Poisonous fish

Some fish use poison to kill their enemies. Many have prickly, poisonous spines. Others have poisonous flesh. Stingrays strike out at their attackers with a poisonous, whiplike tail.

stingray

Blending in

Some fish use camouflage to protect themselves. They blend in with their surroundings so their enemies cannot see them. Some fish look like rocks and some look like seaweed. Many fish have **countershading**. They have a dark-colored back and light-colored belly. When predators look up, the light belly blends in with the sunlight shining above the water. When predators look down, the dark back blends in with the bottom of the river or ocean.

peacock flounder

Four-eyed fish

Have you ever seen a four-eyed fish? One pair of "eyes" is really just circular markings that look like eyes. They are usually located near the back of the body. These false eyes fool predators because they cannot tell which way the fish is swimming.

butterfly fish

Unusual fish

Some types of fish are unusual, or look different from most other fish. Some do not look like fish at all.

Flying fish often "fly" to escape predators such as tuna or dolphins. In the air, however, they are in danger of being captured by an ocean bird such as the albatross.

Flying fish

Some fish can fly! Flying fish live in the open sea. They swim quickly along the surface of the ocean and then thrust themselves out of the water with their tail. They spread their large pectoral fins to glide through the air. Flying fish can fly as high as twenty feet (6 meters) in the air and as far as forty feet (12 meters).

The mudskipper above has climbed up a branch using its pectoral fins like legs. It can stay out of water until it needs new water in its gills.

Mudskippers

Most fish live their entire lives under water, but mudskippers are a type of fish that spend most of their time out of the water. They live in swampy areas. Mudskippers use their pectoral fins to crawl across land to find food. They store extra water in their gills so they can breathe. When the oxygen in the water runs out, the mudskipper must find fresh water for its gills.

Sea horses

Sea horses do not look like most fish. They are tiny fish that grow to be only seven inches (18 cm) long. They swim upright and have small fins on their back to push their body through the water. When sea horses are not swimming, they wrap their tail around tall weeds and sway in the water, hidden from predators.

When sea horses reproduce, the male sea horse is in charge of guarding the eggs. The male keeps the eggs in a pouch on his belly until the tiny sea-horse babies hatch.

Sea dragons

Sea dragons are unusual-looking fish that live in the cool waters around Southern Australia. These fish are named sea dragons because they look so much like the dragons in Chinese **myths**, or stories. Sea dragons grow to be 18 inches (45 cm) long. The female sea dragon lays eggs into a pouch on the male's tail. The male sea dragon carries the eggs in its tail until they hatch.

*This leafy sea dragon hides among seaweed to escape from predators. Its long **appendages**, or external body parts, look like leaves of seaweed.*

Are these fish?

Many creatures that live in the ocean look like fish and are called fish, but they are not fish at all! These animals belong to other groups in the **animal kingdom**.

Are shellfish fish?

Shellfish are actually sea animals called **crustaceans**. They are **invertebrates**. Their body is covered with a hard shell called an **exoskeleton**.

Shrimp, lobsters, crabs, and barnacles are types of crustaceans. This crab lives on the ocean floor. Its soft body is protected by its exoskeleton.

Are dolphins and whales fish?

Dolphins and whales are not fish. They are mammals. These animals live in the ocean, but they do not have gills—they have lungs. They swim to the surface of the water to breathe air. Female mammals give birth to live young and **nurse** their babies with milk from their body.

Are starfish and jellyfish fish?

Jellyfish, shown left, and starfish, shown right, are invertebrates. Starfish are also called sea stars. These animals have unique features to protect their soft body. Jellyfish can sting their prey, as well as their enemies, with their poisonous tentacles. The arms of a starfish are covered with pointed spikes, which make it difficult for some animals to eat them.

Fun fish facts

Fish have many unique ways of surviving under water. Did you know that fish can smell under water and that some fish can glow in the dark?

Smelling under water

Some fish have a strong sense of smell. They can remember specific smells for long periods of time. Salmon are born in freshwater streams and swim to the ocean when they become adults. When salmon are ready to mate, they return to the same stream in which they were born. They find the right stream by remembering the smell of the water.

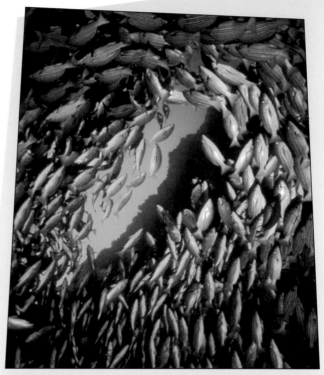

Fish often travel in large groups called **schools** or **shoals**. Schools of fish **migrate**, or travel, to search for food or to find warmer or cooler temperatures.

Glow in the dark

Some fish create their own light! The viperfish, shown left, is a unique fish that lives in the deep sea. Fish that create light have special **cells** lining the sides of their body. The cells produce light, which helps them see in the dark and locate prey. A viperfish uses its large, pointed teeth to catch and eat other fish.

Pollution

Water pollution harms the fish that live in oceans, rivers, and lakes. Factories dump chemicals and other dangerous waste products into rivers. Garbage created by people in towns and cities around the world also gets dumped into the oceans.

Fish have not adapted to pollutants in their environment. They choke on plastic or get trapped in garbage. They absorb chemicals into their body. Many fish die each year due to pollution.

Many species of fish are in danger because their habitats are being destroyed by pollution.

Reefs in danger

Tropical reefs are delicate. They can be damaged easily by storms or by sea creatures that eat coral polyps. Humans, however, are the biggest threat to coral reefs. Garbage and waste chemicals that are dumped in the water kill polyps. Boaters damage tropical reefs by dropping anchor on the coral. People fishing for tropical fish to sell to pet shops also cause damage. They hunt fish using bleach, poison, and dynamite, which are harmful to the reefs.

Some divers damage coral reefs when they break off pieces of coral to take home as souvenirs.

Words to know

animal kingdom The major groups of living things that include every kind of animal

cold-blooded Describing an animal whose body temperature changes with the temperature of its environment

crustacean Sea animals such as shrimp, crabs, and lobsters that have an exoskeleton but do not have a backbone

echinoderms Sea animals such as sea stars that do not have a backbone or head

exoskeleton A hard shell that covers the outside of an invertebrate's body and protects it

food chain A pattern of eating and being eaten

fusiform Describing a shape that is streamlined

habitat The natural place where an animal or plant is found

herbivore An animal that eats mainly plants

invertebrate An animal without a backbone

mate (n) A partner for producing offspring; (v) to reproduce, or make babies

myth A story that is not true

nurse To feed with milk from the body

omnivore An animal that eats both plants and animals

parasite Tiny animals that live on the body of other animals

plankton Tiny plants and animals that live in water and cannot be seen without a microscope or magnifying glass

predators Animals that hunt and eat other animals

species A group of similar living things that can produce offspring together

sperm A male reproductive cell

tide The changing level of the water in oceans

vertebrate An animal with a backbone; the bones that make up a backbone are called vertebrae

warm-blooded Describing an animal whose body temperature stays the same regardless of the temperature of its environment

Index

9 0 Printed in the U.S.A. 7 6 5